The art of healthy food

Super Juicing

igloobooks

igl003books

Published in 2016
by Igloo Books Ltd
Cottage Farm
Sywell
NN6 0BJ
www.igloobooks.com

Food photography and recipe development
© StockFood, © The Food Media Agency
Additional imagery © iStock / Getty Images
Cover image © iStock / Getty Images

Cover designed by Nicholas Gage
Edited by Bobby Newlyn-Jones

HUN001 1016
2 4 6 8 10 9 7 5 3 1
ISBN 978-1-78670-250-0

Printed and manufactured in China

Contents

Introduction

'You are what you eat,' or so the saying goes. Never before has this been so true, in an age where it is all too easy to overfill our bodies with processed foods, refined carbohydrates and additives. Yet what if the things we eat are fresh, tasty, appetising and full of goodness? It really is possible to make this change to our diets – and juicing is a quick, simple and enjoyable way to do so.

Juice and more

Modern-day juicing is so much more than simply extracting the juice from fruit. Armed with a decent juicer that can handle the tough stuff (such as carrots and pineapple skins), you can create delicious and nutritious concoctions. These tasty drinks can add another dimension to your diet – substitute a healthy juice in place of a naughty snack. If you cannot forgo the snacks, add a low-calorie juice, too! A juice shot is an excellent way to kick-start your day. If you are on a real health kick, there are options for total 'juice cleansing' programmes, with regimes lasting from a single day to a whole week of juice-only nutrition. Juicing can change your relationship with food for the better.

Why Juice?

What's so great about juicing? Why not just eat a few more raw carrots, add some spinach to your evening meal and make sure you help yourself as you walk past the fruit bowl, instead of reaching for the 'naughty treats' cupboard?

Five-a-day is the way

Put simply, adding a single juice to your daily food intake can help you reach your five-a-day target of fruit and vegetables more easily. Juices contain only raw ingredients, so fewer minerals and vitamins are lost than during the cooking process.

Juice benefits

Juices can make a difference to what you see on the outside and how you feel on the inside. There are juice recipes to boost immunity, lift your energy levels and help you refuel after exercise. The right juices can lead to clearer skin, stronger teeth and nails, reduced allergies and better sleep.

How it works

Why are vegetables and fruit thought to be of more benefit in their liquid form?
Juicing ambassadors claim that they can boost a sluggish digestive system,
allowing your body to absorb many more nutrients than it would if you crunched
on an apple or picked your way through a plateful of curly kale.

Less technically, juicing also allows you to consume far larger amounts of healthy vegetables than if you had to sit and eat them. It is also easier to mix it up, introducing a variety of foods that you would not include as part of a meal or to take in foods that do not appeal to you. You can disguise individual tastes when they are blended in a cocktail of fruit-and-vegetable deliciousness.

Keeping it in

Juicing retains more than 90 per cent of the nutrients in fruit and vegetables.

Juicing to lose weight

Small but juicy changes to your daily diet can have great health effects – but what if your main goal is weight loss? There are two approaches: the first is to cut out all the foods you know are bad for you (because no matter how we justify it, a slice of carrot cake is an indulgence, not a slimming aid), and replace them instead with vibrant, vital nutrients in juice form. This can be a slow but steady way to drop pounds gradually, over weeks and months. Research shows that it works and you will feel cleansed and energised in the process.

Juicing to cleanse

The second approach involves a more radical attack on body fat, the 'juice cleanse'. Advocates of juice cleanses say that if the ingredients are chosen carefully, the right mixture of juices can sustain your body for days at a time, without taking on board any other foods. There are several cleansing programmes available, including DIY plans found in books or online. There are also plans where you order everything for your cleanse and it comes ready to drink.

Cleanse, not fast

A juice cleanse is not a 'fast'. You are not cutting out food, merely choosing to take in calories and nutrients through juice alone. Ensure that you drink 1.6 litres (3 ½ pints) of water each day.

Each type of plan should provide you with regular juice 'meals' and sufficient calories for your body to function without impairment. You will find that you are 'eating' every two to three hours to stave off hunger pangs and keep your energy levels topped up. Some programmes recommend sticking to your usual exercise regime, while others suggest you limit yourself to light exercise, such as walking and yoga. Be sensible in your approach: if you are a marathon runner you will not want to lose your levels of fitness but may have to reduce your daily distance. If you're not an exercise junkie, do not suddenly throw yourself into a new cycle of boxing and bootcamps – listen to your body!

Body Basics

Generally speaking, people juice for one of three reasons: to bump up their intake of nutrients, to cleanse or detox their body or to lose weight. How does juicing, rather than simply eating lots of fruit and vegetables, work?

Busting toxins?

Proponents of the juice cleanse – drinking juice, water and nothing else – claim that it will rid your body of toxins and deliver a host of nutrients to your body in their most readily digestible form. Their theory is that the juicing process predigests the food for you, giving your gut a rest and allowing your body to preserve energy that it would normally use during the digestive process. However, there are those that refute these claims. There are concerns that juicing diminishes the amount of nutrients and fails to provide healthy levels of fibre, protein and the right fats. It is argued that the whole notion of 'detoxing' is redundant, as the body has its own systems in place to do exactly that. They warn also about the dangers of cutting down calories to the point that your metabolism slows, or the weight piles straight back on when you start eating normally again. This book takes into account all of this information, and will guide you on the safest and most effective way to enjoy juices.

Goodness in a glass

What experts do all agree on is that juicing, in
moderation, can have its benefits. A fresh juice made
from organic vegetables is always going to be a healthy
alternative to pizza. Drinking freshly-squeezed juice
will certainly boost your intake of fruit and vegetables,
especially if you are the kind of person who avoids the
green bits in meals. Smoothies, which use the whole
fruit, are a good compromise as long as they do not
increase your calorie intake by too much. Juicing is also
a great way to take a look at what you are putting inside
your body, and ultimately, to feel like you are controlling
your food rather than the other way round.

Home and Away

There is much talk these days about the hidden dangers of fruit juices and smoothies. Some research claims that they contain high levels of natural sugars, are lacking in fibre and can cause spikes in blood sugar levels, plus their sweet taste can lead to an addiction to sugary foods and can dull sensitivity to sweetness. So why undertake a new lifestyle that advocates drinking fruit juice?

Taking control of the contents

The answer is simple: your home-made juices will be nothing like the juices you buy at the supermarket or coffee shop. By making your own juices, you are taking control of what is in them. Your juices should be biased towards vegetables, with fruits contributing to a smaller percentage of your daily intake. Additionally, your recipes will retain more fibre than shop-bought juices. Fibre slows down your digestion (keeping you fuller for longer) and the amount of natural sugars that are absorbed.

Buyer beware!

Treat yourself at a smoothie bar, and you are likely to be buying a glorified milkshake containing fruit concentrates instead of whole fruit. This lowers the vitamin values of the drinks. They commonly have high sugar levels and a large calorie count. Cartons of juice and smoothies are often pasteurised to extend their shelf-life and contain a whole list of additives. They simply are not the same as the freshly juiced recipes you can make for yourself. Grab a juice on the go from a juice bar, and you will also pay a high price, whether it's healthy or not. The simple rule is to prepare your own juices at home so you know exactly what you are getting. You have bought the produce, you've chosen what you add, and after reading this book, you will know the benefits you are getting out.

Keep it quick

Juices are best drunk within 20 minutes of making them; after that, their nutritional value begins to drop.

Fitting It In

The secret to successful, enjoyable juicing is making it work for your lifestyle. There is no denying it: juicing at home (rather than buying pre-prepared juices) can be messy and seemingly a lot of preparation to make a small amount of juice. Taking juices out and about to fit your timetable can be tricky. However, with some careful preparation and planning, it can be done.

Some juices, and most smoothies, can be prepared in advance and taken out with you. You will need a decent flask to keep them cool, and may find you have to stir them if they have separated into a foamy layer with clearer liquid underneath.

Juicing for a day

If you embark upon a whole day juice-fest (that is fest, not fast!) you should find
that you are actually in the kitchen for less time than you usually are. It takes
around ten minutes to prepare a juice and clean up afterwards. Compare that to
the hour that passes trying to put together a nutritiously balanced main course,
or 20 minutes spent perusing the shelves until you settle for beans on toast.

Can I still exercise?

Not only can you still exercise, but you must. Any plan that cuts out exercise is
an unhealthy one. If you are supplementing your normal diet with juices, then
you should find your energy levels are boosted, not reduced. Several ingredients
included in the recipes will actually be of benefit when you exercise. The juices are
a natural, healthy, isotonic alternative to calorie-laden 'sports drinks', which may
be packed with artificial sweeteners, preservatives and other chemicals.

In addition, juices provide much-needed fluids to replace those lost during sporting
activity. They contain carbohydrates in a lower-fibre, lower-bulk form that are
quickly taken on board. They also provide nutrition when you need it the most
in a tasty, palatable way, when you may find that you have killed your appetite
by exercising.

Side Effects

If you have chosen to drink nothing but juices for a day or two, you may find your body reacting in unexpected ways. Hunger is a distracting side effect. Headaches are a common complaint, and you may feel more fatigued than you usually do. Stick with it, because these symptoms are your body's way of recalibrating, and you will get through it. If your symptoms do not desist within two days or after returning to solid food, then you should see your doctor.

Beating a headache

Headaches most commonly occur because you have cut out caffeine and refined sugar. Try not to resort to tablets; after all, you are focusing on a cleaner, healthier body. Instead, get active. The endorphins released when you move your body are natural painkillers, and working out can boost oxygen flow through your body and blood flow to your brain. Ginger is also a natural headache remedy, relaxing the blood vessels and relieving tension, so add some to your juice.

Eat your greens

Many people are surprised to find that once their bodies are used to juices, they are not actually hungry. However, if you are, there are ways and means of beating hunger pangs. Firstly, try to 'chew' your veggie-based juices – it feels more like you are eating normally. If necessary, mimic your everyday eating patterns. Serve your juice in a bowl and eat it like soup. Sit at the table and read, or chat with your family, just as you would with a plate of food in front of you. Try not to grab your juice on the go, but make it into a mealtime like any other food.

Kick-start your system

Chewing your juice stimulates your salivary glands, which in turn warn your stomach to expect a food parcel pretty soon. The brain sends messages to your digestive system, warning it of the type of food that is on its way.

Getting Started

You will be able to make some of the recipes in this book with just a blender, but for most you will need a good quality juicer. Once you have that, your shopping list will consist mostly of fresh fruit and vegetables; buy organic where possible. If you plan to drink your juices on the move, you will also need a vacuum flask (to keep them fresh) or a leak-free sports bottle.

Which juicer is best?

There are so many juicers on the market nowadays, it's hard to know which one to buy. If you can afford it, go for at least a mid-price model; you really do get what you pay for. The main choice is between centrifugal or masticating juicers.

Centrifugal juicers use a rapidly spinning sieve basket with a serrated cutting blade at the bottom to separate the juice from the pulp. They are noisy but faster to use, and easier to clean and store than masticating juicers. Try to buy one with a large feeder tube, so you spend less time chopping your ingredients to fit into the machine.

Ice is nice

Most fresh juices benefit from being served cold, so stock up on ice; try keeping ice cubes in a paper bag in your freezer to stop them from sticking together.

If budget is not a problem, you may want to invest in a masticating juicer. Also known as slow-speed or cold-press juicers, they produce less heat, which reduces the oxidation of the juice – meaning it retains more nutrients. It also means you will be able to store your juice for much longer (sometimes up to 48 hours). However, you will end up spending more time making your juices as the feeder chute is generally smaller. Masticating juicers can be extremely pricey, but often come with extra attachments for making ice cream, extracting pasta, grinding coffee or mincing. Fans of this type of juicer will also tell you that the juices retain more pulp, meaning they have more fibre and even some protein. The thicker consistency allows you to chew on your juice or water it down a little for drinking.

The Garden Gang

You may be surprised at how many fruits and vegetables can be juiced. Each has its own benefits. Some boost the nutritional value of a recipe, while others add sweetness to prevent a juice being overly bitter or earthy.

Carrots Every juicer's friend, carrots are bursting with goodness. Juicing carrots benefits your body by making beta-carotene more available and absorbed more efficiently than eating them raw.

Apples These will form the bulk of many recipes, especially on a juice-cleanse. Avoid Granny Smiths as they do not juice well. Apples are a great antioxidant and their sweet, zingy taste compliments other less-palatable ingredients.

Pineapples Another fruit that bulks out your juices; a quarter of a pineapple will add several ounces to your drink. They can be very sweet, but if you juice the skins, this will counteract the sweetness. The flesh adds a satisfying thickness if you blend a little into your juice at the end.

Leafy greens You have probably read a lot about 'leafy greens' as a general term. The term is a catch-all for kale, chard, spinach, collard greens, rapini, bok choi, green cabbage, and even such leaves as dandelion greens and romaine lettuce. They add vitamins and minerals by the bucketload and can make you feel like you are drinking the healthiest option of all the juices.

Ginger It is neither fruit nor vegetable but it works really well in juices. It does not need to be peeled, but use it sparingly as it has a very powerful taste. It has so many health benefits, helping to tame nausea, treat colds, fight off infection and it acts as an antiseptic and antihistamine, among many other things.

Beetroot This root has a powerful effect on the appearance of your juices, and also on your body. It helps your body fight against many complaints. It is something of an acquired taste, variably described as sweet and delicious or tasting a little like dirt.

It's a no-no

Banana, avocado, papaya and similar soft fruits don't juice at all well. They do, however, boost your juices, so can be mixed with the juice at the end of the process in a blender or liquidiser.

Supplements

One of the main arguments against the health benefits of juicing is that it cuts out valuable elements of your food, such as fibre and calcium. If you are simply adding a juice shot at the start of the day, or using a smoothie as a tasty snack or post-exercise pick-me-up, then you have no need to worry. If, however, you are using juices as your main food source during a cleanse or detox programme, you should consider supplementing the juices with certain other items.

Wheatgrass Fans of juicing constantly sing the praises of this gloriously green stuff. Described as 'liquid sunshine', it gets its vibrant green from the high levels of chlorophyll it contains. Among the many benefits claimed are its powers to fight off colds and fevers and to improve digestion and cleanse the system. It is said to be a powerful antioxidant. It can be juiced on its own and drunk as a shot, or added to other juices in fresh or powdered form. It is worth noting that centrifugal juicers cannot extract juice from fresh wheatgrass.

Psyllium husk This high-fibre ingredient is suggested on week-long juice cleanses to prevent constipation and keep the intestine and bowel functioning properly. It is mixed into the juices. Alternatively, ground chia seeds can be added to your recipes to increase the fibre levels, and also contribute to your levels of omega-3 fatty acids, protein and antioxidants.

Probiotics Said to have a beneficial effect on the gut, probiotics ('friendly' bacteria, such as acidophilus) supplement the body's own naturally occurring micro-organisms within the digestive system. They can be bought as freeze-dried powders, capsules and tablets and added to your juices and smoothies. Alternatively, make your smoothies with bio-live yogurt.

Spirulina Usually sold as powder or flakes, spirulina comes from blue-green algae, which is nutritionally rich in vitamins and minerals, with some protein and fatty acids. It can be tricky to mix into juices, so use a blender as the final stage of your preparation.

Nuts A great form of protein and fibre, nuts can be juiced in a masticating juicer after soaking overnight in filtered water. Strain off the soaking water and juice with an equal amount of nuts and fresh water. The nut milk is especially delicious when used in smoothies. Try to use fresh, raw (unpasteurised) nuts such as almonds, hazelnuts, walnuts and pecans.

Cut It Out

While you are treating your body to the benefits of juices, you should consider what else you are putting into your system. Try to cut out any drinks that you know are counter-effective: the worst culprits are coffee, alcohol and sugary squash or fizzy drinks. You will really ring the changes if you increase the amount of water you drink each day.

Fancy a brew?

There are several drinks you can substitute if you want something other than water. Herbal teas are caffeine-free and offer their own benefits beyond quenching your thirst. If you fancy a fruit tea, check the packet before you boil the kettle. Many fruit teas are blended from synthetic ingredients to give them their fruitiness.

The best approach is to brew your own. Start the day with lemon tea by simply putting a slice of lemon in a cup with hot (not boiling) water. Most citrus fruits make delicious tea, but the vitamin content can be quashed by using boiling water.

At the end of the day, try chamomile tea or fennel tea. Fennel has an aniseed taste and many health bonuses: it is a diuretic and has anti-spasmodic properties that will relax the intestinal muscles, making it good for constipation or flatulence. You can make it from fennel seeds (crush and cover with hot water) or use fennel stalks steeped in hot water.

Fresh peppermint tea is a wonderful aid to digestion and also good before bedtime. Experiment with different mint leaves to see if you have a personal preference: apple mint and spearmint both work well but have subtly different tastes.

Sack the sodas

Fizzy drinks are the complete antithesis of healthy juices. They are high-calorie concoctions of dyes, preservatives, corn syrup, sweeteners and sometimes BVO (brominated vegetable oil), which is linked to nerve disorders and memory loss (and is used to make some plastics flame retardant).

How to Juice

If the only juice you are used to is that from freshly-squeezed oranges, then juicing is going to be something of a shock. Don't worry about the time-consuming act of peeling, coring or chopping. One of the beauties of these juices is just how easy they are to put together.

Preparation? What preparation?

You can juice most fruit and vegetables without much preparation. Wash them and chop them into chunks to suit the size of your juicer. You can juice unwaxed citrus peel, pineapple skins, apple cores, carrot tops and celery leaves. However, you should not juice or blend fruit stones (peach, nectarine and apricot stones may produce symptoms of cyanide poisoning) and avocado and banana skins. The biggest hassle is the cleaning and washing up, and getting rid of the pulp and sticky stains. However, get into good juicing habits as follows:

- Line the pulp collection container with a bag before you begin

- Run a sink full of hot, soapy water

- Prepare your juice, pour it into a glass and put it in the fridge

- Tidy up before you drink: throw out the bag of pulp, wipe down sticky surfaces and wash your juicer

Don't be lazy

Don't fall into the trap of leaving your dishwasher to do your dirty work. It might leave the jug section of your juicer spotless, but it will not work well on the mesh.

Shop savvy

Where possible, buy organic fruit and vegetables because you will be juicing the whole thing, skins and all. Choose fruits at the peak of their ripeness for the highest nutritional value. Avoid anything bruised, over-ripe or not ripe enough. Under-ripe fruits are tougher on the digestive system. Where possible, stick to local, in-season produce. This is a better guarantee of quality; out-of-season crops may have been forced to ripeness and over-fertilised.

The Comedown

You may work your way slowly into a more healthy, juicy lifestyle, finding that it's not so hard after all. Or you may hurtle headlong into your new juicing regime, casting aside all solids. Whatever your approach, it is important to plan ahead for the days when you reintroduce solid food to your meal times.

Beating the cravings

Some people crave specific foods after a juice cleanse. However, your body needs a gentle reintroduction to foods that genuinely, properly need chewing. The chances are, if you rush straight out and devour a three-course meal at a great restaurant, you are going to suffer for it afterwards.

Begin by grazing on small meals consisting mostly of salads and fruit. Soup will continue your diet of easy-to-digest, vitamin-rich, vegetable-based foodstuffs. Do not tackle dairy, meat or starchy carbohydrates too soon (give it a couple of days at least) and even then, start with brown rice and steamed fish. Try to keep up the good work by snacking on raw, unsalted nuts and raw vegetables. Think of the goodness you have put into your body, and try not to go back to your old habits of eating ready meals or giving in to takeaways.

Slowly does it

Eat your food slowly – not just on your first days back after a juice cleanse, but all the time. Take smaller bites, chew for longer and really savour the food in your mouth. This will help your digestion and your enjoyment of food, and reduce stress levels in today's 'do it all, do it fast, do it now' society. You should also find that you eat less overall; your brain needs 20 minutes to register that you are feeling full, so give it that time before you overeat without even realising.

You Can Do It

There may be times when you wonder why you have embarked on this crazy way of 'eating'. Be strong and take stock of how you are feeling.

Is it really hunger?

If the overriding sensation is one of hunger, then ask yourself: are you really hungry, or are you just craving foods that you have declared forbidden for the time being? A juice cleanse really *does* provide all you need to fuel your body but it does not satisfy the need for chocolate, stodge or those oh-so-good-on-your-tongue fats that you would normally allow yourself in moments of weakness.

A healthy choice

You may ask yourself if you have to do this. You have chosen to up your intake of foods that you know are good for you and to decrease the amount of 'bad stuff' you are putting into your body, and you are doing it in a tasty, novel way. Focus on the choices you are making while you pulverise another carrot. Would you sit down and eat four apples and two carrots in one go? Unlikely – and yet with ten minutes' preparation time, you can have those exact foods in a delicious drink.

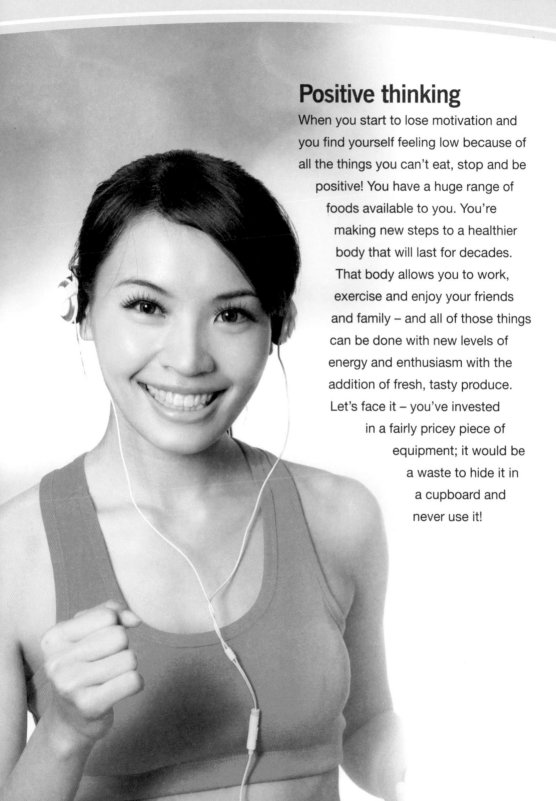

Positive thinking

When you start to lose motivation and you find yourself feeling low because of all the things you can't eat, stop and be positive! You have a huge range of foods available to you. You're making new steps to a healthier body that will last for decades. That body allows you to work, exercise and enjoy your friends and family – and all of those things can be done with new levels of energy and enthusiasm with the addition of fresh, tasty produce. Let's face it – you've invested in a fairly pricey piece of equipment; it would be a waste to hide it in a cupboard and never use it!

A Closer Look

Your body requires a whole range of nutrients to keep it functioning properly. Choose recipes containing different vegetables and fruit to take in a wide variety of nutrients according to your needs. Each recipe highlights which nutrients are gained from the ingredients.

Body benefits: minerals

Calcium	Vital for strong bones and teeth, helps to regulate heartbeat, benefits muscle function, nerve transmissions and hormone secretion
Chlorine	Improves liver function, balances fluids in the body, helps produce digestive juices in the stomach
Iodine	Good for healthy skin, nails and hair, assists the thyroid gland, important for energy and growth
Iron	Helps the blood carry oxygen around the body, used for making protein and enzymes, builds muscles
Magnesium	Good for a healthy heart and muscles, needed for bone growth, boosts immunity
Manganese	Helps bones grow and cells function, aids the metabolism of carbohydrates and fats
Phosphorus	Balances body hydration, moves muscles, regulates heartbeat and delivers nutrients to cells, good for strong teeth and bones
Potassium	Maintains heart rhythm and pH balance of blood, used to build proteins, breaks down and uses carbohydrates, good for kidneys, blood pressure, circulation and nerves

Selenium (with vit. E)	Prevents cell damage, enhances liver function, protects against cancer and heart disease, is a powerful antioxidant
Sodium	Balances water in blood and tissue, stimulates muscle and nerve function; too much can lead to high blood pressure, so do not add extra salt to your juices
Sulphur	Good for skin, hair, nails and brain and liver function
Zinc	Helps wounds heal, aids hormone and liver function, is an antioxidant

Don't lose it

Your body will try to expel excess sodium (salt). During this process, it binds with calcium, meaning that you will lose a much-needed mineral during the process. That's why we should all keep salt (added during or after cooking, or hidden in processed foods) to a healthy intake level.

What is an antioxidant?

Antioxidants take various forms and are found in many foods. They help to counteract nasties known as 'free radicals' that are generated in many ways (for example, pollution, smoking, stress, pesticides and drugs). The free radicals have too few electrons and so steal electrons from other molecules, causing damage to our bodies' cells. Studies suggest that antioxidant supplements may be of little benefit, but those consumed in foods such as berries have a large part to play in keeping us healthy.

Body benefits: vitamins

A (beta-carotene)	The body converts beta-carotene into vitamin A and then uses it to build strong teeth and bones, boost the immune system and protect the digestive and respiratory systems, it is a strong antioxidant
B1 (thiamine)	Keeps muscles and nerves healthy, helps break down food to release energy
B2 (riboflavin)	Important for healthy skin, eyes, nails and hair, helps release energy from carbohydrates
B3 (niacin)	Releases energy from food, good for digestion and the nervous system
B5 (pantothenic acid)	Helps release energy from food
B6 (pyridoxine)	Allows the body to store and use energy from carbohydrates and protein, good for skin and blood
B9 (folic acid)	Used to make red blood cells, repair DNA and avoid tumour growth and genetic disorders
C (ascorbic acid)	Protects cells, helps wounds heal, needed for healthy tissue, guards against disease, is a powerful antioxidant
D (from sunlight)	You can't eat it, but you can exercise to get it or spend time outdoors. Vital for healthy bones and teeth, helps absorb calcium and phosphorus
E	Protects cells, prevents premature ageing, helps the immune system and circulation, is a powerful antioxidant
K	Needed for blood clotting so helps wounds heal, also good for bone strength

Food stores

Your body can store fat-soluble vitamins (A, D, E and K), so your daily requirement does not necessarily need a daily intake. However, water-soluble vitamins (vitamin B-complex and vitamin C), most often found in fruit and vegetables (and grains) are not stored, so you must have them more frequently. Any excesses are lost when you urinate. It is vital that you vary your diet to get the whole range of vitamins and minerals.

Going Veggie

Going Veggie

Vegetable-based juices pack the biggest nutritional punch with fewer calories and sugars, depending upon the juices you choose. Root vegetables can be higher in sugar than other vegetables but they are still lower than many fruits.

Choose your recipes for their vibrant appearance and tantilising tastes, but also for their properties. Carrots and spinach are an excellent source of beta-carotene, which is good for your eyes and is a great antioxidant.

Many recipes call for small additions of fruit to your vegetable juices to temper the taste, sweeten them and to add new textures.

Ones to watch

Look out for these icons with each recipe.
They list the main benefits from the selection of ingredients.

 = skin booster 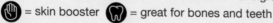 = great for bones and teeth

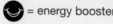 = energy booster 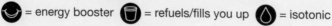 = refuels/fills you up = isotonic

Carrot and Cabbage Juice

Serves: 4
Preparation time: 10 minutes

Ingredients

6 medium carrots, peeled
1 large Hispi cabbage, shredded
1 orange, juiced
150 ml / 5 fl. oz / ⅔ cup cold water
150 g / 5 oz / ⅔ cup crushed ice

Method

1. Pass the carrots and cabbage through a juicer; collect the juice.

2. Add the juice to a blender with the orange juice, water and crushed ice.

3. Blitz until smooth before passing through a fine sieve into glasses.

4. Serve immediately or cover and chill for up to 1 hour.

Super-green Juice

Serves: 4
Preparation time: 10 minutes

Ingredients

6 sticks of celery, peeled

1 large cucumber, sliced

1 large head of iceberg lettuce, shredded

1 lime, juiced

a pinch of salt

250 g / 9 oz / 1 cup crushed ice

Method

1. Pass the celery, cucumber and lettuce through a juicer; collect the juice.

2. Combine the juice with the lime juice, salt and crushed ice in a blender.

3. Blitz until smooth before passing through a sieve into glasses.

4. Serve immediately.

Beetroot and Broccoli Juice

Serves: 4
Preparation time: 10 minutes
Cooking time: 5 minutes

Ingredients

1 small head of broccoli, prepared into small florets

4 small cooked beets, chopped

a pinch of salt

150 ml / 5 fl. oz / ⅔ cup cold water

110 g / 4 oz / ½ cup crushed ice

Method

1. Bring a saucepan of water to a simmer; place the broccoli in a steaming basket and sit atop the saucepan.

2. Steam for 3–4 minutes until just tender. Remove and add to a blender with the beets, salt, water and crushed ice.

3. Blitz until smooth before passing through a sieve into a jug.

4. Pour into glasses and serve immediately.

Avocado Smoothie

Serves: 4
Preparation time: 5 minutes

Ingredients

100 g / 3 ½ oz / 2 cups watercress

1 medium ripe avocado, pitted and flesh chopped

1 large cucumber, chopped

150 ml / 5 fl. oz / ⅔ cup soy or almond milk

a pinch of salt

250 g / 9 oz / 1 cup crushed ice

Method

1. Combine the watercress, avocado, cucumber and milk in a blender; blitz until smooth.

2. Add the crushed ice and salt and blitz again until smooth.

3. Pour into glasses and serve immediately.

Gazpacho

Serves: 4
Preparation time: 2 hours 10 minutes

Ingredients

300 g / 10 ½ oz / 2 cups vine tomatoes,
   cored and chopped

1 large cucumber, chopped

4 sticks of celery, peeled

2 red peppers, chopped

1 green pepper, chopped

a pinch of salt and pepper

1 lime, juiced

250 g / 9 oz / 1 cup crushed ice

Method

1. Pass the tomatoes, cucumber, celery and peppers through a juicer; collect the juice.

2. Combine the juice with a pinch of seasoning, lime juice and the crushed ice in a blender.

3. Blitz until smooth before straining into a jug.

4. Cover and chill for 2 hours before serving.

3-Veggie Smoothie

Serves: 4
Preparation time: 10 minutes

Ingredients

6 medium carrots, peeled

4 sticks of celery, peeled

55 g / 2 oz / 1 cup baby spinach leaves, washed

110 g / 4 oz / ½ cup plain yogurt

250 g / 9 oz / 1 cup crushed ice

Method

1. Pass the carrots and celery sticks through a juicer; collect the juice.

2. Combine the juice with the spinach leaves, yogurt and ice in a blender.

3. Blitz until smooth before pouring into glasses.

4. Serve immediately for best results.

Tomato Cocktail

Serves: 4
Preparation time: 3 hours 5 minutes

Ingredients

300 g / 10 ½ oz / 2 cups cherry
    tomatoes, halved

1 large cucumber, thinly sliced

1 l / 1 pint 16 fl. oz / 4 cups cold water

½ lime, juiced

a pinch of salt

350 g / 12 oz / 1 ½ cups ice cubes

Method

1. Mix together the tomatoes, cucumber slices, water, lime juice and salt in a jug.

2. Churn with a bar spoon for 30 seconds; cover and chill for 3 hours.

3. After chilling, pour into ice-filled glasses and serve.

Beet Smoothie

Serves: 4
Preparation time: 10 minutes

Ingredients

1 large globe artichoke, peeled and trimmed

1 lemon, juiced

3 small cooked beets, chopped

2 large carrots, peeled

3 sticks of celery, peeled

150 ml / 5 fl. oz / ⅔ cup almond milk

2 tsp wheatgrass powder

250 g / 9 oz / 1 cup crushed ice

Method

1. Rub the artichoke with the lemon juice before passing through a juicer along with the beets, carrots and celery; collect the juice.

2. Combine the juice with the almond milk, wheatgrass powder and ice in a blender; blitz until smooth.

3. Pour into glasses and serve immediately for best results.

Barley Juice

Serves: 4
Preparation time: 10 minutes

Ingredients

4 medium carrots, peeled

4 large Braeburn apples, cored and chopped

4 small cooked beets, chopped

a small handful of mint leaves

110 ml / 4 fl. oz / ½ cup aloe vera juice

2 tsp barley juice powder

½ tsp wheatgrass powder

250 g / 9 oz / 1 cup crushed ice

Method

1. Pass the carrots, apples and beets through a juicer; collect the juice.

2. Combine the juice with the mint leaves, aloe vera juice, barley juice and wheatgrass powder in a blender.

3. Blitz until smooth before adding the crushed ice.

4. Blitz again before pouring into glasses; serve immediately for best results.

Celery Smoothie

Serves: 4
Preparation time: 10 minutes

Ingredients

4 large carrots, peeled

4 sticks of celery, peeled

1 apple, cored and chopped

55 g / 2 oz / 1 cup baby spinach, washed

1 orange, juiced

250 g / 9 oz / 1 cup crushed ice

Method

1. Pass the carrots, celery and apple through a juicer; collect the juice.

2. Add the juice to a blender with the spinach, orange juice and crushed ice; blitz until smooth.

3. Pass the juice through a fine sieve into a jug.

4. Pour into glasses and serve immediately for best results.

Broccoli Smoothie

Serves: 4
Preparation time: 10 minutes

Ingredients

2 small heads of broccoli, prepared into small
   florets

2 Granny Smith apples, cored and chopped

150 g / 5 oz / 3 cups baby spinach

110 g / 4 oz / ½ cup plain yogurt

1 tsp wheatgrass powder

250 g / 9 oz / 1 cup crushed ice

Method

1. Pass the broccoli and apple through
a juicer; collect the juice.

2. Combine the juice with the spinach, yogurt,
wheatgrass powder and crushed ice in a
blender.

3. Blitz until smooth before pouring
into glasses.

4. Serve immediately for best results.

Cucumber Smoothie

Serves: 4
Preparation time: 10 minutes

Ingredients

1 large cucumber, sliced

4 carrots, peeled

1 large ripe avocado, pitted and flesh
   chopped

1 orange, juiced

110 ml / 4 fl. oz / ½ cup almond milk

250 g / 9 oz / 1 cup crushed ice

Method

1. Pass the cucumber and carrots through
a juicer; collect the juice.

2. Combine the juice with the avocado,
orange juice, almond milk and crushed ice in
a blender.

3. Blitz until smooth before pouring into short
glasses and serving.

Tomato, Celery and Cucumber Smoothie

Serves: 4
Preparation time: 10 minutes

Ingredients

250 g / 9 oz / 1 ²/₃ cups cherry
   tomatoes, halved

2 small cucumber, peeled and chopped

4 sticks of celery, peeled

½ orange, juiced

75 g / 3 oz / ¹/₃ cup plain yogurt

250 g / 9 oz / 1 cup crushed ice

Method

1. Pass the tomatoes, cucumber and celery through a juicer; collect the juice.

2. Combine the juice with the orange juice yogurt and crushed ice in a blender; blitz until smooth.

3. Pour into glasses and serve immediately for best results.

Green Pepper Smoothie

Serves: 4
Preparation time: 10 minutes
Cooking time: 2 minutes

Ingredients

1 small head of broccoli, prepared into florets

2 green peppers, diced

1 green chilli (chili) pepper, chopped

150 ml / 5 fl. oz / ²⁄₃ cup almond milk

250 g / 9 oz / 1 cup crushed ice

Method

1. Bring a large saucepan of salted water to the boil; add the broccoli and blanch for 2 minutes before draining.

2. Add the broccoli florets to a blender along with the chopped peppers, chilli pepper, almond milk and crushed ice.

3. Blitz until very smooth; pour into glasses and serve.

Red Pepper and Ginger Smoothie

Serves: 4
Preparation time: 10 minutes

Ingredients

2 red peppers, chopped
5 cm (2 in) piece of root ginger, peeled
4 medium carrots, peeled
a pinch of Cayenne pepper
110 g / 4 oz / ½ cup plain yogurt
250 g / 9 oz / 1 cup crushed ice

Method

1. Pass the peppers, ginger and carrots through a juicer; collect the juice.

2. Combine the juice with the Cayenne pepper, yogurt and crushed ice in a blender; blitz until smooth.

3. Pour into glasses and serve immediately for best results.

Cucumber and Kiwi Smoothie

Serves: 4
Preparation time: 5 minutes

Ingredients

2 large cucumbers, chopped

2 kiwi fruit, peeled and diced

250 g / 9 oz / 1 cup plain low-fat yogurt

250 g / 9 oz / 1 cup crushed ice

a pinch of salt

Method

1. Combine the cucumber and kiwi fruit in a blender; blitz until slushy.

2. Add the yogurt and ice and blitz again until liquid and smooth.

3. Pour into glasses and serve immediately for best results.

Fennel Smoothie

Serves: 4
Preparation time: 5 minutes
Cooking time: 3–4 minutes

Ingredients

250 g / 9 oz / 1 ²/₃ cups asparagus spears, woody ends removed

1 large cucumber

1 bulb of fennel, thinly sliced

1 lime, juiced

150 ml / 5 fl. oz / ²/₃ cup cold water

175 g / 6 oz / ¾ cup crushed ice

Method

1. Place a steaming basket over a saucepan of simmering water; add the asparagus to the basket and steam for 3–4 minutes until just tender.

2. Chop and add to a blender with the cucumber, fennel, lime juice, water and crushed ice.

3. Blitz until smooth before passing through a sieve into a jug.

4. Pour into glasses and serve immediately.

Lettuce and Tomato Juice

Serves: 4
Preparation time: 10 minutes

Ingredients

400 g / 14 oz / 2 ⅔ cups cherry
    tomatoes, halved

2 heads of Romaine lettuce, chopped

2 cucumbers, peeled and chopped

a pinch of salt

325 g / 11 oz / 1 ⅓ cups crushed ice

Method

1. Pass the cherry tomatoes, lettuce
and cucumber through a juicer; collect
the juice.

2. Add the juice and a pinch of salt to a
blender along with the crushed ice.

3. Blitz until smooth before pouring into
glasses and serving.

Tomato and Carrot Juice

Serves: 4
Preparation time: 10 minutes

Ingredients

300 g / 10 ½ oz / 2 cups cherry tomatoes on the vine, picked and chopped

4 medium carrots, peeled

4 sticks of celery, peeled

1 orange, juiced

250 g / 9 oz / 1 cup crushed ice

Method

1. Pass the tomatoes, carrots and celery through a juicer; collect the juice.

2. Combine the juice with the orange juice and crushed ice in a blender.

3. Blitz until smooth before pouring into glasses and serving.

Celery and Watermelon Juice

Serves: 4
Preparation time: 5 minutes
Cooking time: 5 minutes

Ingredients

½ watermelon, peeled and cut into chunks

4 sticks of celery, peeled and chopped

1 orange, juiced

½ lime, juiced

250 g / 9 oz / 1 cup crushed ice

Method

1. Combine the watermelon, celery, orange and lime juices and crushed ice in a blender.

2. Blitz until smooth; pour into glasses and serve immediately for best results.

Vegetable Milkshake

Serves: 4
Preparation time: 5–10 minutes

Ingredients

2 red peppers, chopped

2 green peppers, chopped

300 g / 10 ½ oz / 2 cups vine tomatoes,
  cored and chopped

225 g / 8 oz / 1 cup plain yogurt

375 ml / 13 fl. oz / 1 ½ cups soy milk

55 g / 2 oz / 1 cup watercress

½ tsp wheatgrass powder

a pinch of salt

250 g / 9 oz / 1 cup crushed ice

Method

1. Combine the peppers, tomatoes, yogurt, milk and most of the watercress in a blender.

2. Blitz until smooth before adding the wheatgrass powder, salt and crushed ice.

3. Blitz again until combined; pour into glasses and serve with the remaining watercress on top as a garnish.

Carrot and Pomegranate Juice

Serves: 4
Preparation time: 10 minutes

Ingredients

4 medium carrots, peeled

300 g / 10 ½ oz / 2 cups white
seedless grapes

1 pomegranate, halved with seeds removed

1 lemon, juiced

250 g / 9 oz / 1 cup crushed ice

Method

1. Pass the carrots and grapes through a juicer; collect the juice.

2. Combine the collected juice with the pomegranate seeds, lemon juice and crushed ice in a blender.

3. Blitz until smooth before passing through a fine sieve into a jug.

4. Pour into glasses and serve immediately for best results.

Carrot Zinger

Makes: 200 ml
Preparation time: 5 minutes

Ingredients

3 large carrots, sliced

2 medium oranges, quartered

1 knob ginger

Method

1. Process the ingredients through an electronic juicer followed by the pineapple, according to the manufacturer's instructions.

2. Pour into a bottle and shake until thoroughly mixed.

Feeling Fruity

Feeling Fruity

It is obvious by their taste that some fruits are sweeter than others. Lemons are lower in sugar than oranges, for example. Choose which fruit recipes you are going to try by their ingredients and the health benefits that you particularly require: an energy boost, to ward off a cold or to improve digestion.

If you are trying to cut down on sugar, even those found in fruit, lower-sugar fruits include berries such as blueberries, blackberries and raspberries, and citrus fruits such as grapefruit, lemons and limes.

Some fruits, including blackberries and apricots, produce relatively small amounts of juice. Juice recipes may be bulked up by the addition of watery produce such as cucumber and celery.

Apple and Pear Smoothie

Serves: 4
Preparation time: 5 minutes

Ingredients

2 Granny Smith apples, cored and chopped
2 Rocha pears, cored and chopped
1 head of iceberg lettuce, shredded
250 ml / 9 fl. oz / 1 cup skimmed milk
125 g / 4 ½ oz / ½ cup ice cubes

Method

1. Blitz together the apple, pear, lettuce and milk in a food processor until smooth.

2. Add the ice cubes and blitz again until the smoothie is chilled.

3. Pass the liquid through a sieve into a jug; cover and chill until ready to serve.

Ginger, Lime and Fresh Mint Juice

Serves: 4
Preparation time: 2 hours 5 minutes

Ingredients

10 cm (4 in) piece of root ginger, peeled

2 limes, juiced

2 tbsp agave nectar

1 l / 1 pint 16 fl. oz / 4 cups cold water

a small bunch of mint leaves

Method

1. Finely grate the ginger before mixing with the lime juice, agave nectar, cold water and most of the mint in a large jug.

2. Stir well, cover, and chill for 2 hours.

3. After two hours, strain the liquid through a fine sieve into glasses.

4. Garnish with the remaining mint before serving.

Strawberry and Bilberry Juice

Serves: 4
Preparation time: 5 minutes

Ingredients

300 g / 10 ½ oz / 2 cups strawberries, hulled

150 g / 5 oz / 1 cup seedless red grapes

150 g / 5 oz / 1 cup bilberries (use blueberries if not available)

a few drops of vanilla extract

250 g / 9 oz / 1 cup crushed ice

Method

1. Combine the strawberries, grapes, bilberries, vanilla extract and crushed ice in a blender.

2. Blitz until smooth before pouring into glasses.

3. Serve immediately or cover and chill for up to 1 hour.

Pineapple Smoothie

Serves: 4
Preparation time: 5 minutes

Ingredients

1 medium pineapple, peeled and cored
250 g / 9 oz / 1 $^2/_3$ cups strawberries, hulled
2 medium bananas, chopped
150 g / 5 oz / $^2/_3$ cup strawberry yogurt
250 g / 9 oz / 1 cup crushed ice

Method

1. Chop the pineapple flesh and combine it with the strawberries, banana and yogurt in a blender.

2. Blitz until smooth before adding the crushed ice; blitz again.

3. Pour into glasses and serve immediately.

Papaya Smoothie

Serves: 4
Preparation time: 5–10 minutes

Ingredients

1 small pineapple, peeled and cored
1 ripe papaya, deseeded and flesh chopped
1 large ripe mango, pitted and flesh chopped
1 lime, juiced
110 g / 4 oz / ½ cup plain yogurt
250 g / 9 oz / 1 cup crushed ice

Method

1. Chop the pineapple flesh before adding to a blender along with the papaya, mango, lime juice and yogurt.

2. Blitz until smooth before adding the crushed ice; blitz again.

3. Pour into glasses and serve immediately.

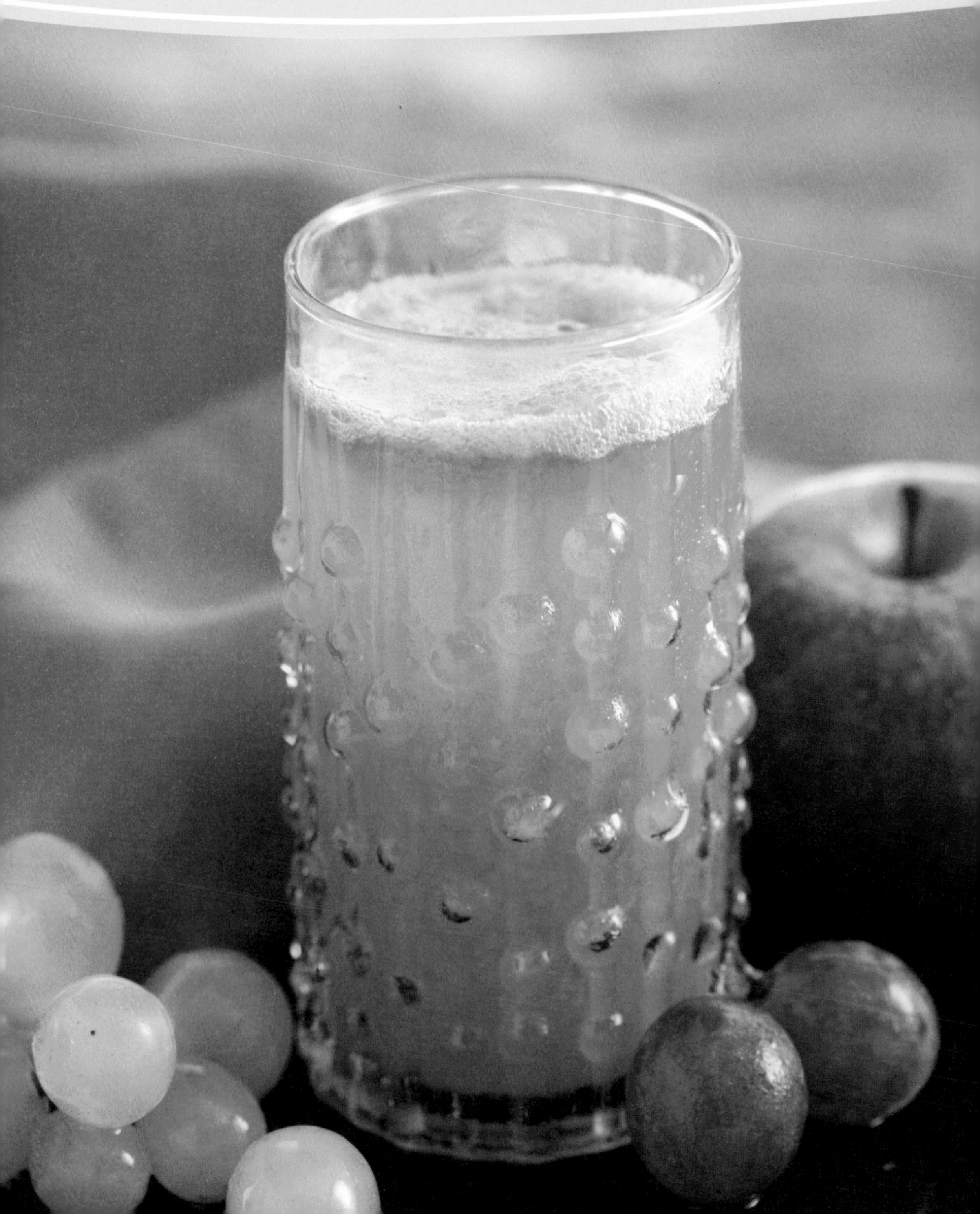

Grape Smoothie

Serves: 4
Preparation time: 10 minutes

Ingredients

2 large gala apples, cored and chopped

200 g / 7 oz / 1 ⅓ cups white
   seedless grapes

200 g / 7 oz / 1 ⅓ cups red
   seedless grapes

250 g / 9 oz / 1 cup crushed ice

Method

1. Pass the apples and grapes through a juicer; collect the juice.

2. Combine the juice and crushed ice in a blender and blitz until smooth.

3. Pass through a sieve into glasses before serving.

Glass of Melon Juice

Serves: 4
Preparation time: 10 minutes

Ingredients

2 charentais melons
a pinch of salt
250 g / 9 oz / 1 cup crushed ice

Method

1. Quarter the melons and discard the seeds before roughly chopping the flesh.

2. Sprinkle a pinch of salt over the flesh before blitzing in a blender until smooth; pass through a sieve back into the blender.

3. Add the crushed ice and blitz again until smooth.

4. Pass through a fine sieve into glasses before serving.

Pineapple Juice

Serves: 4
Preparation time: 5–10 minutes

Ingredients

2 small pineapples, peeled and cored

5 cm (2 in) piece of root ginger, peeled and grated

a small bunch of mint leaves, roughly chopped

a few drops of vanilla extract

350 g / 12 oz / 1 ½ cups crushed iced

Method

1. Roughly chop the pineapple flesh and add to a blender along with the grated ginger, mint leaves and vanilla extract.

2. Blitz until pulpy; add the crushed iced and blitz again until smooth.

3. Pass through a fine sieve into a jug before pouring into glasses and serving.

Peach Smoothie

Serves: 4
Preparation time: 10 minutes

Ingredients

2 ripe peaches, pitted and chopped
2 Braeburn apples, cored and chopped
300 g / 10 ½ oz / 2 cups raspberries
110 g / 4 oz / ½ cup raspberry yogurt
250 g / 9 oz / 1 cup crushed ice

Method

1. Pass the peach and apple through a juicer;
collect the juice.

2. Combine the juice with the raspberries,
raspberry yogurt and crushed ice in a
blender; blitz until smooth.

3. Pour into glasses and serve immediately.

Grapefruit Smoothie

Serves: 4
Preparation time: 5 minutes

Ingredients

2 pink grapefruit, segmented

2 medium bananas, chopped

1 large ripe mango, pitted and
  flesh chopped

1 lime, juiced

150 g / 5 oz / ⅔ cup plain yogurt

250 g / 9 oz / 1 cup crushed ice

Method

1. Combine the pink grapefruit, banana,
mango, lime juice and yogurt in
a blender.

2. Blitz until smooth before adding the
crushed ice; blitz again.

3. Pour into glasses and serve immediately.

Lime and Raspberry Juice

Serves: 4
Preparation time: 1 hour 5 minutes

Ingredients

6 limes
300 g / 10 ½ oz / 2 cups raspberries
1 l / 1 pint 16 fl. oz / 4 cups cold water
2 tbsp agave nectar
250 g / 9 oz / 1 cup ice cubes

Method

1. Halve four of the limes and juice into a jug.

2. Add the raspberries, water and agave nectar; churn with a bar spoon for 30 seconds before covering and chilling for 1 hour.

3. After 1 hour, slice the remaining limes thinly and add to the jug with the ice cubes.

4. Stir briefly before serving.

Watermelon Juice

Serves: 4
Preparation time: 10 minutes

Ingredients

1 large watermelon, deseeded and diced
½ lime, juiced
250 g / 9 oz / 1 cup crushed ice
a pinch of salt

Method

1. Combine the watermelon and lime juice in a blender; blitz until smooth, working batches if necessary.

2. Pass the juice through a sieve and back into the blender.

3. Add the ice and a pinch of salt before blitzing again until smooth and frothy.

4. Pour into glasses and serve immediately for best results.

Apricot Smoothie

Serves: 4
Preparation time: 5–10 minutes

Ingredients

1 medium pineapple, peeled and cored
4 ripe apricots, pitted
1 lime, juiced
250 g / 9 oz / 1 cup crushed ice

Method

1. Chop the pineapple flesh and apricots before adding to a blender with the lime juice.

2. Blitz until smooth before adding the crushed ice and blitzing again until smooth.

3. Pass the smoothie through a sieve into a jug before pouring into glasses and serving.

Watermelon and Lime Juice

Serves: 4
Preparation time: 10 minutes

Ingredients

6 limes
½ watermelon, flesh cubed
2 tbsp agave nectar
600 g / 1 lb 5 oz / 2 ½ cups crushed ice

Method

1. Halve 4 of the limes and juice them into a blender.

2. Add the watermelon flesh, agave nectar and half of the crushed ice; blitz until smooth before passing through a sieve into a jug.

3. Slice the remaining limes and arrange them in ice-filled glasses.

4. Pour over the juice and serve immediately for best results.

Peach Juice

Serves: 4
Preparation time: 10 minutes

Ingredients

1 l / 1 pint 16 fl. oz / 4 cups cold water
4 ripe peaches, pitted and chopped
2 tbsp runny honey
a small handful of mint leaves, chopped

Method

1. Combine 250 ml / 8 oz / 1 cup of water with half of the chopped peaches and honey in a food processor.

2. Blitz until smooth before adding the remaining water.

3. Blitz again before pouring into a jug; stir through the remaining peaches and chopped mint.

4. Cover and chill before serving.

Redcurrant Smoothie

Serves: 4
Preparation time: 10 minutes

Ingredients

2 Granny Smith apples, cored and sliced

225 g / 8 oz / 1 ½ cups seedless red grapes

225 g / 8 oz / 2 cups redcurrants

110 g / 4 oz / ½ cup plain yogurt

250 g / 9 oz / 1 cup crushed ice

Method

1. Pass the apples, grapes and redcurrants through a juicer; collect the juice.

2. Combine the juice with the plain yogurt and crushed ice in a blender; blitz until smooth.

3. Pour into glasses and serve immediately.

Summer Fruits and Orange Juice

Serves: 4
Preparation time: 10 minutes

Ingredients

6 oranges, segmented
110 g / 4 oz / 1 cup redcurrants
100 g / 3 ½ oz / ²/₃ cup raspberries
110 g / 4 oz / ½ cup vanilla yogurt
250 g / 9 oz / 1 cup crushed ice

Method

1. Blitz together the orange segments, redcurrants and raspberries in a blender; pass through a fine sieve back and back into the blender.

2. Add the yogurt and crushed ice; blitz again until smooth.

3. Pour into glasses and serve immediately for best results.

Melon and Kiwi Smoothie

Serves: 4
Preparation time: 5 minutes

Ingredients

6 kiwi fruit, peeled and chopped

1 small Galia melon, deseeded and flesh
  chopped

½ lemon, juiced

a few drops of vanilla extract

250 g / 9 oz / 1 cup crushed ice

Method

1. Combine the kiwi fruit, melon, lemon juice
and vanilla extract in a blender.

2. Blitz until smooth before adding the
crushed ice and blitzing again.

3. Pour into glasses and serve immediately
for best results.

Mango Juice

Serves: 4
Preparation time: 5 minutes

Ingredients

2 ripe mangoes, pitted

1 lime, juiced

1 tsbp agave nectar

250 g / 9 oz / 1 cup crushed ice

Method

1. Roughly chop the mango flesh before adding to a blender along with the lime juice, agave nectar and crushed ice.

2. Blitz until smooth before passing through a sieve into glasses.

3. Serve immediately for best results.

Peach, Orange and Lemon Juice

Serves: 4
Preparation time: 1 hour 5 minutes

Ingredients

4 ripe peaches, pitted and chopped

4 oranges, juiced

2 lemons, juiced

1 tbsp agave nectar

a few drops of vanilla extract

250 g / 9 oz / 1 cup crushed ice

a few sprigs of red basil, to garnish

Method

1. Combine the peach, orange juice, lemon juice, agave nectar, vanilla extract and crushed ice in a blender.

2. Blitz until smooth; pass through a fine sieve into a jug.

3. Cover and chill for up to 1 hour.

4. Pour the juice in glasses and garnish with red basil before serving.

Orange and Papaya Juice

Serves: 4
Preparation time: 10 minutes

Ingredients

4 oranges, segmented
2 ripe papayas, deseeded and flesh
   chopped
1 lemon, juiced
250 g / 9 oz / 1 cup crushed ice
a small handful of mint leaves, to garnish

Method

1. Blitz together the orange segments, papaya flesh and lemon juice in a blender.

2. Pass the juice through a sieve and back into the blender.

3. Add the crushed ice and blitz again until smooth.

4. Pour into glasses and garnish with mint leaves on top.

5. Serve immediately for best results.

Orange and Banana Juice

Serves: 4
Preparation time: 5–10 minutes

Ingredients

2 large ripe bananas, chopped

4 oranges, segmented

1 tbsp honey

250 g / 9 oz / 1 cup crushed ice

Method

1. Blitz together the chopped bananas, orange segments, honey and crushed ice in a blender until smooth.

2. Pour through a sieve into a jug before pouring into glasses.

3. Serve immediately for best results.

Watermelon and Dill Juice

Serves: 4
Preparation time: 5–10 minutes

Ingredients

250 g / 9 oz / 1 cup crushed ice
250 ml / 9 fl. oz / 1 cup cold water
½ lime, juiced
½ watermelon, flesh cubed
2 tbsp agave nectar
a small bunch of dill, chopped

Method

1. Combine the ice, water, lime juice and watermelon in a blender.

2. Blitz until smooth before adding the agave nectar and two tablespoons of chopped dill.

3. Blitz again before passing through a sieve into a jug.

4. Garnish with more dill before serving.

Blueberry Smoothie

Serves: 4
Preparation time: 5 minutes

Ingredients

300 g / 10 ½ oz / 2 cups strawberries,
   hulled and chopped

200 g / 7 oz / 2 cups blueberries

250 ml / 9 fl. oz / 1 cup skimmed milk

250 g / 9 oz / 1 cup low-fat strawberry yogurt

Method

1. Combine all the ingredients in a blender and blitz until smooth.

2. Stir well before pouring into a jug; cover and chill until ready to serve.

3. This smoothie is best served as soon after making as possible.

Apple, Berry and Grapefruit Juice

Serves: 4
Preparation time: 10 minutes

Ingredients

3 pink grapefruit, segmented with
  pith removed

2 Granny Smith apples, cored and chopped

75 g / 3 oz / ½ cup bilberries (use blueberries
  if not available)

2 sticks of celery, peeled and chopped

250 g / 9 oz / 1 cup crushed ice

Method

1. Pass the pink grapefruit flesh, apple,
bilberries and celery through a juicer; collect
the juice.

2. Combine the juice and crushed ice in a
blender and blitz until smooth.

3. Pass through a fine sieve into a jug.

4. Cover and chill or serve immediately for
best results.

Grape, Celery and Pineapple Juice

Serves: 4
Preparation time: 10 minutes

Ingredients

8 sticks of celery, peeled and chopped

1 head of iceberg lettuce, shredded

1 small pineapple, peeled, cored and diced

300 g / 10 ½ oz / 2 cups white seedless grapes

250 g / 9 oz / 1 cup crushed ice

Method

1. Pass the celery and lettuce through the juicer, collecting the juice.

2. Follow with the pineapple and grapes; pass the juice from the fruit through a sieve before combining with the celery and lettuce juice in a blender.

3. Add the crushed ice and blitz until smooth.

4. Pour into glasses and serve immediately for best results.

Watermelon Refresher

Makes: 375 ml
Preparation time: 5 minutes

Ingredients

450 g / 1 lb / 3 cups watermelon, peeled
  and diced

150 g / 5 ½ oz / 1 cup raspberries

6 mint leaves, plus a few more to garnish

2 apples, cut into chunks

Method

1. Process the ingredients in the order shown
through an electronic juicer, according to the
manufacturer's instructions.

2. Serve the juice garnished with mint leaves.

Blackcurrant Smasher

Makes: 450 ml
Preparation time: 10 minutes

Ingredients

2 apples, cut into chunks

1 fennel bulb, cut into chunks

75 g / 2 ½ oz / ½ cup blackcurrants

2 ripe avocados, peeled and stoned

2 tsp agave nectar

mint leaves to garnish

Method

1. Process the apple and fennel through an electronic juicer, according to the manufacturer's instructions.

2. Transfer the juice to a liquidiser and add the blackcurrants, avocado and agave nectar.

3. Blend until smooth, adding a handful of ice cubes to chill if preferred. Pour into glasses and serve immediately, garnished with mint.

Tropical Temptation

Makes: 525 ml
Preparation time: 5 minutes

Ingredients

2 ripe mangoes, stoned and cut into chunks

1 pineapple, peeled and cut into chunks

Method

1. Process the mangoes through an electronic juicer followed by the pineapple, according to the manufacturer's instructions.

2. Stir vigorously with a spoon to mix, then pour into glasses and serve immediately.

Kiwi and Banana Blitz

Makes: 275 ml
Preparation time: 5 minutes

Ingredients

8 kiwi fruit
2 ripe bananas, peeled and sliced

Method

1. Process the kiwi fruit through an electronic juicer, according to the manufacturer's instructions.

2. Transfer the juice to a liquidiser and add the banana.

3. Blend until smooth, adding a handful of ice cubes to chill if preferred. Serve immediately.

Super Smoothies

Super Smoothies

Smoothies are a great way to increase your energy levels, in particular before or after exercise, when you just do not feel like cooking a meal. Most smoothie recipes contain a source of calcium such as yoghurt, milk or quark. You will need a blender to make the smoothie recipes, and they are best served chilled or over ice.

Many smoothies are naturally higher in calories than straight juices, so one a day is a good guideline. Bananas are one of the highest-sugar fruits and differ greatly in size too, so do not overindulge if you are on a serious calorie-controlled diet.

Smoothies can be made out of season using tinned or dried fruits – but watch the calorie count. Try adding frozen fruits such as berries, which work well in smoothies.

Cabbage and Pear Smoothie

Serves: 4
Preparation time: 5–10 minutes

Ingredients

3 Conference pears, cored and chopped
½ head of white cabbage, shredded
4 sticks of celery, peeled and chopped
250 ml / 9 fl. oz / 1 cup fresh apple juice
125 g / 4 ½ oz / ½ cup crushed iced

Method

1. Pass the pears, cabbage and celery through a juicer; collect the juice.

2. Combine the pressed juice with the apple juice and crushed ice in a blender.

3. Blitz until smooth; pass through a sieve into a jug.

4. Cover and chill until ready to serve.

Peach, Avocado and Kiwi Smoothie

Serves: 4
Preparation time: 5 minutes

Ingredients

2 kiwi fruit, peeled and chopped

4 ripe peaches, pitted and chopped

1 small ripe avocado, pitted and chopped

1 lime, juiced

75 ml / 3 fl. oz / 1/3 cup skimmed milk

110 g / 4 oz / 1/2 cup plain low-fat yogurt

125 g / 4 1/2 oz / 1/2 cup crushed ice

Method

1. Combine the kiwi fruit, peach, avocado, lime juice, milk and yogurt in a blender; blitz until smooth.

2. Add the crushed ice and blitz again until combined.

3. Pour the smoothie into four small glasses and serve immediately.

Watermelon and Bilberry Smoothie

Serves: 4
Preparation time: 5–10 minutes

Ingredients

½ watermelon, peeled and cut into chunks

225 g / 8 oz / 1 ½ cups bilberries (use blueberries if not available)

2 large cucumbers, roughly chopped

150 g / 5 oz / ⅔ cup crushed ice

Method

1. Blitz together the watermelon, bilberries and cucumber in a blender.

2. Pass through a sieve back into the blender before adding the crushed ice.

3. Blitz again until chilled; cover and chill before serving.

Mandarin Smoothie

Serves: 4
Preparation time: 5 minutes

Ingredients

2 Comice pears, cored and chopped
4 mandarins, peeled and segmented
4 apricots, pitted and chopped
125 ml / 4 ½ fl. oz / ½ cup fresh orange juice
250 g / 9 oz / 1 cup crushed ice

Method

1. Combine the pear, mandarin segments, apricot, orange juice and crushed ice in a blender.

2. Blitz until smooth before passing through a fine sieve into a jug.

3. Pour into short glasses and serve immediately.

Strawberry Smoothie

Serves: 4
Preparation time: 5 minutes

Ingredients

2 Conference pears, cored and chopped

300 g / 10 ½ oz / 2 cups strawberries,
hulled and chopped

225 g / 8 oz / 1 ½ cups black cherries, pitted

250 g / 9 oz / 1 cup crushed ice

Method

1. Combine the pears, strawberries and cherries in a blender; blitz until smooth.

2. Add the crushed ice and blitz again before pouring into glasses.

3. Serve immediately for best results.

Peach and Raspberry Smoothie

Serves: 4
Preparation time: 5–10 minutes

Ingredients

2 ripe peaches, pitted and chopped

300 g / 10 ½ oz / 2 cups raspberries

2 Cox or gala apples, cored and sliced

1 lime, juiced

1 lemon, juiced

250 g / 9 oz / 1 cup crushed ice

Method

1. Pass the peach, raspberries and apple through a juicer; collect the juice.

2. Combine the juice with the lime and lemon juices in a blender.

3. Stir well and add the crushed ice; blitz until smooth.

4. Pour into glasses and serve immediately.

Watermelon and Strawberry Smoothie

Serves: 4
Preparation time: 5 minutes

Ingredients

½ watermelon, peeled and cut into chunks

300 g / 10 ½ oz / 2 cups strawberries, hulled
and chopped

1 lime, juiced

110 g / 4 oz / ½ cup plain yogurt

250 g / 9 oz / 1 cup crushed ice

a few sprigs of basil, chopped

Method

1. Combine the watermelon, strawberries,
lime juice and yogurt in a blender.

2. Blitz until smooth; add the crushed ice
and blitz again briefly until the ice has
mostly dissolved.

3. Pour into glasses and top with a sprinkle
of basil before serving.

Tomato, Mint and Orange Smoothie

Serves: 4
Preparation time: 5 minutes

Ingredients

225 g / 8 oz / 1 ½ cups cherry
   tomatoes, halved

6 medium oranges, peeled and segmented

a small bunch of mint, roughly chopped

250 g / 9 oz / 1 cup crushed ice

a pinch of salt

extra sprigs of mint, to garnish

Method

1. Combine the cherry tomato halves, orange segments, chopped mint, crushed ice and a pinch of salt in a blender.

2. Blitz until smooth; pass through a sieve into a jug.

3. Pour into glasses and garnish with mint sprigs before serving.

Passion Fruit and Papaya Smoothie

Serves: 4
Preparation time: 5–10 minutes

Ingredients

3 passion fruit, halved

1 papaya, deseeded with flesh chopped

2 golden delicious apples, cored and chopped

125 ml / 4 ½ fl. oz / ½ cup fresh orange juice

1 lime, juiced

250 g / 9 oz / 1 cup crushed ice

Method

1. Add the passion fruit, papaya, apple, orange and lime juices; blitz until smooth before passing through a sieve back into the blender.

2. Add the crushed ice and blitz again until smooth.

3. Pour into glasses and serve immediately.

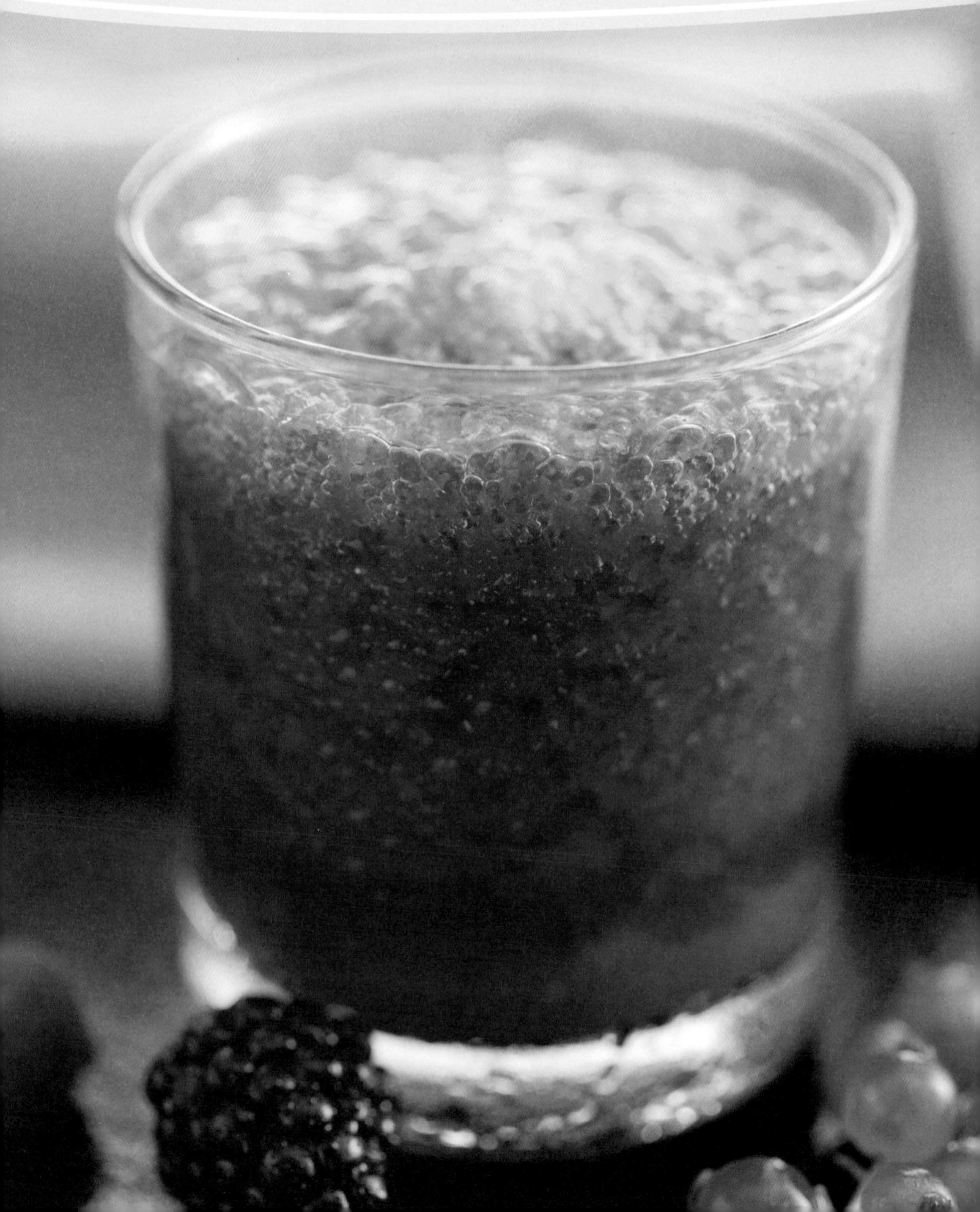

Summer Fruit Smoothie

Serves: 4
Preparation time: 5 minutes

Ingredients

150 g / 5 oz / 1 cup strawberries, hulled and chopped

150 g / 5 oz / 1 cup blackberries

150 g / 5 oz / 1 cup raspberries

110 g / 4 oz / 1 cup redcurrants

350 g / 12 oz / 1 ½ cups crushed iced

a drop of vanilla extract

Method

1. Combine all the ingredients in a blender; blitz until slushy.

2. Pour into glasses and serve immediately for best results.

3. Alternatively, you can cover and chill the smoothie for up to 2 hours before serving for a thinner consistency.

Pomegranate, Kiwi and Lime Smoothie

Serves: 4
Preparation time: 5 minutes

Ingredients

6 kiwi fruit, peeled and chopped

1 pomegranate, halved and deseeded

2 limes, juiced

110 g / 4 oz / ½ cup plain yogurt

250 g / 9 oz / 1 cup crushed ice

Method

1. Combine the kiwi fruit, most of the pomegranate seeds, lime juice, yogurt and crushed ice in a blender.

2. Blitz until smooth; pour into glasses.

3. Top with the remaining pomegranate seeds before serving.

Beetroot, Apple and Carrot Juice

Serves: 4
Preparation time: 5–10 minutes

Ingredients

2 medium carrots, peeled and cut into
large pieces

150 g / 5 oz / 1 cup cooked beetroot, cubed

2 Granny Smith apples, cored and chopped

1 orange, juiced

250 g / 9 oz / 1 cup crushed ice

Method

1. Pass the carrots, beetroot and chopped apple through a juicer; collect the juice.

2. Combine the pressed juice with the orange juice and crushed ice in a blender.

3. Blitz until smooth before passing through a fine sieve into a jug.

4. Cover and chill until ready to serve in short glasses.

Blueberry Soother

Makes: 400 ml
Preparation time: 10 minutes

Ingredients

3 medium beetroot, cut into chunks

2 oranges, peeled

100 g / 3 ½ oz / 2/3 cup blueberries, plus extra to garnish

1 large ripe banana, peeled

mint leaves to garnish

Method

1. Process the beetroot and orange through an electronic juicer, according to the manufacturer's instructions.

2. Transfer the juice to a liquidiser and add the blackberries and banana.

3. Blend until smooth, adding a handful of ice cubes to chill if preferred. Pour into glasses and serve immediately, garnished with blueberries and mint leaves.

Summertime Smoothie

Makes: 500 ml
Preparation time: 10 minutes
Freezing time: 3 hours

Ingredients

450 g / 1 lb / 3 cups mixed summer berries

½ cantaloupe melon, peeled and cut
   into chunks

1 cucumber, cut into chunks

Method

1. Spread the berries out on a baking tray and freeze for 3 hours or until solid.

2. Process the cantaloupe and cucumber through an electronic juicer, according to the manufacturer's instructions.

3. Transfer the juice to a liquidiser and add the frozen berries. Blend until smooth, then pour into glasses and serve immediately.

Healthy Blends

Healthy Blends

The juices in this section will help anyone on a cleansing juice regime get a good mixture of nutrients from a single drink. They take a whole variety of ingredients and blitz the juices together for their varying qualities, from the minerals and vitamins they contain to the amount of protein and monounsaturated fat (from avocado) and carbohydrates (in bananas) they supply to your body.

Some ingredients are included in minimal amounts but really make a difference, both to the taste of your juice and to the power blast it provides. Ginger is a great example of this: a small amount makes a big impact on the taste of the juice, and the root has an extremely long list of curative qualities and benefits.

Beetroot, Apple and Ginger Juice

Serves: 4
Preparation time: 10 minutes

Ingredients

6 small cooked beets

4 large Braeburn apples, cored and chopped

5 cm (2 in) piece of root ginger, peeled

2 limes, juiced

250 g / 9 oz / 1 cup crushed ice

Method

1. Pass the beets, apple and root ginger through a juicer; collect the juice.

2. Combine the juice with the lime juice and crushed ice in a blender.

3. Blitz until smooth before pouring into glasses.

4. Serve immediately.

Pineapple and Celery Smoothie

Serves: 4
Preparation time: 10 minutes

Ingredients

1 small pineapple, peeled and cored

4 sticks of celery, peeled

2 small iceberg lettuce, shredded

55 ml / 2 fl. oz / ¼ cup aloe vera juice

1 lime, juiced

1 tbsp agave nectar

110 g / 4 oz / ½ cup plain yogurt

250 g / 9 oz / 1 cup crushed ice

Method

1. Chop the pineapple flesh and pass through a juicer with the celery and lettuce; collect the juice.

2. Combine the juice with the aloe vera juice, lime juice, agave nectar, yogurt and crushed ice; blitz until smooth.

3. Pour into glasses and serve immediately for best results.

Carrot, Beets and Strawberry Cooler

Serves: 4
Preparation time: 10 minutes

Ingredients

4 medium carrots, peeled

4 small cooked beets, chopped

300 g / 10 ½ oz / 2 cups strawberries, hulled

2 oranges, juiced

250 g / 9 oz / 1 cup crushed ice

Method

1. Pass the carrots and beets through a juicer; collect the juice.

2. Combine the juice with the orange juice and crushed ice in a blender; blitz until smooth.

3. Pass the juice through a sieve into glasses and serve immediately.

Tomato and Grapefruit Smoothie

Serves: 4
Preparation time: 5 minutes

Ingredients

250 g / 9 oz / 1 ²/₃ cups vine tomatoes, cored and chopped

4 pink grapefruit, segmented

1 hispi cabbage, shredded

250 g / 9 oz / 1 cup plain yogurt

250 g / 9 oz / 1 cup crushed ice

Method

1. Blitz together the tomatoes, pink grapefruit and cabbage in a blender until smooth.

2. Add the yogurt and crushed ice and blitz again before pouring into glasses.

3. Serve immediately for best results.

Turnip Juice Smoothie

Serves: 4
Preparation time: 10 minutes

Ingredients

6 medium carrots, peeled

2 turnips, peeled and chopped

75 g / 3 oz / 1 ½ cups baby spinach, washed

a pinch of salt

175 ml / 6 fl. oz / ¾ cup almond milk

250 g / 9 oz / 1 cup crushed ice

Method

1. Pass the carrots and turnips through a juicer; collect the juice.

2. Combine the juice with the spinach, salt, almond milk and crushed ice in a blender.

3. Blitz until smooth before pouring into glasses and serving.

Goji Berry Smoothies

Serves: 8
Preparation time: 10 minutes
Cooking time: 8–10 minutes

Ingredients

250 g / 9 oz / 2 cups cranberries

2 tbsp dried Goji berries

1 lime, juiced

250 ml / 9 fl. oz / 1 cup cold water

110 g / 4 oz / ½ cup plain yogurt

250 g / 9 oz / 1 cup crushed ice

Method

1. Combine the cranberries, goji berries, lime juice and water in a small saucepan.

2. Cook over a medium heat, covered, for 8–10 minutes until the cranberries are soft and starting to burst.

3. Remove from the heat and leave to cool for 5 minutes before blitzing with the yogurt and crushed ice in a blender.

4. Pour into tall shot glasses and serve immediately.

Cucumber and Carrot Juice

Serves: 4
Preparation time:
2 hour 10 minutes

Ingredients

2 large cucumbers, chopped

4 small carrots, peeled and chopped

a small bunch of coriander (cilantro), chopped

a pinch of salt and pepper

1 lime, juiced

250 g / 9 oz / 1 cup crushed ice

Method

1. Pass the cucumbers and carrots through a juicer; collect the juice.

2. Combine the juice with the coriander, a pinch of seasoning, lime juice and the crushed ice in a blender.

3. Blitz until smooth before straining into a jug.

4. Cover and chill for 2 hours before serving.

Carrot, Peach and Apricot Juice Cooler

Serves: 4
Preparation time: 10 minutes

Ingredients

6 medium carrots, peeled

extra carrots, to garnish

3 large peaches, pitted and chopped

4 ripe apricots, pitted and halved

250 g / 9 oz / 1 cup crushed ice

1 lemon, juiced

Method

1. Pass the carrots, peaches and apricots through a juice; collect the juice.

2. Combine the juice with the crushed ice and lemon juice in a blender.

3. Blitz until smooth before pouring into glasses and garnishing with carrots.

Strawberry Dream

Makes: 500 ml
Preparation time: 10 minutes

Ingredients

400 g / 14 oz / 3 cups parsnip, sliced

½ honeydew melon, peeled and cut into chunks

150 g / 5 ½ oz / 1 cup strawberries

1 ripe banana, peeled

Method

1. Process the parsnip and melon through an electronic juicer, according to the manufacturer's instructions.

2. Transfer the juice to a liquidiser and add the strawberries and banana.

3. Blend until smooth, adding a handful of ice cubes to chill if preferred. Pour into glasses and serve immediately.

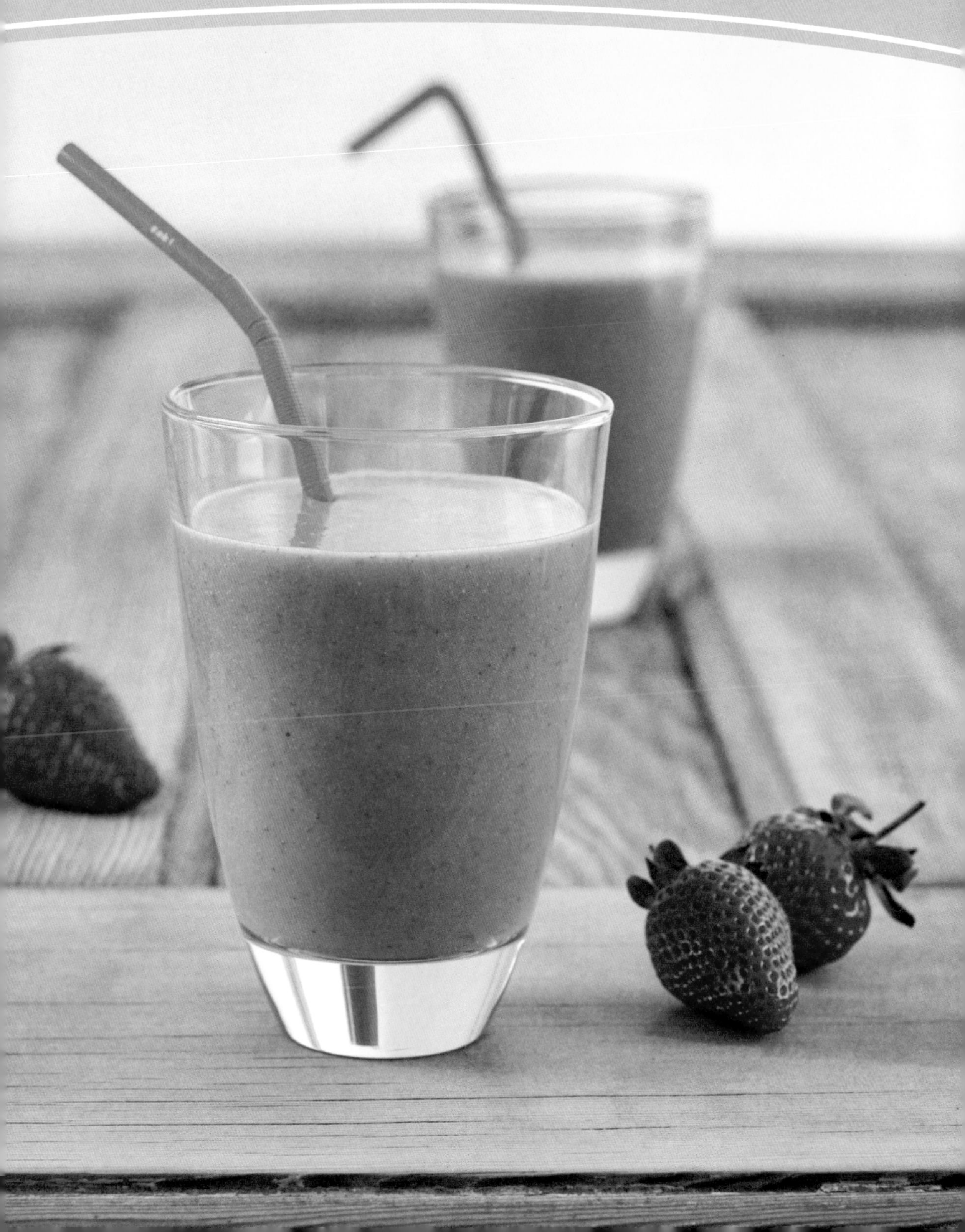

Icy Avocado Calmer

Makes: 400 ml
Preparation time: 10 minutes
Freezing time: 3 hours

Ingredients

2 ripe avocados, peeled, stoned and cut into chunks

150 g / 5 ½ oz / 1 cup green seedless grapes

1 cucumber, cut into chunks

1 romaine lettuce, cut into chunks

1 lime, halved with 1 slice reserved for the garnish

4 mint leaves

Method

1. Spread the avocado and grapes out on a baking tray and freeze for 3 hours or until solid.

2. Process the cucumber, lettuce and lime through an electronic juicer, according to the manufacturer's instructions.

3. Transfer the juice to a liquidiser and add the mint leaves, the frozen avocado and grapes. Blend until smooth, then pour into a glass and garnish with a slice of lime.

Strawberry Linseed Shake

Makes: 400 ml
Preparation time: 10 minutes
Freezing time: 3 hours

Ingredients

2 ripe bananas, peeled and sliced

150 g / 5 ½ oz / 1 cup strawberries, hulled

2 papaya, cut into chunks and
    seeds removed

3 pink grapefruit, peeled

1 tbsp golden linseeds, plus an extra sprinkle
    to garnish

mint to garnish

Method

1. Spread the banana and strawberries out on a baking tray and freeze for 3 hours or until solid.

2. Process the papaya and grapefruit through an electronic juicer, according to the manufacturer's instructions.

3. Transfer the juice to a liquidiser and add the linseeds and frozen fruit. Blend until smooth, then pour into a glass and garnish with mint and an extra sprinkle of linseeds.

Dear Diary

Dear Diary

So, what's it to be? Are you going to augment your diet with a selection of delicious shots and smoothies, or are you ready for a full-on juice cleanse?

Either way, you should chart your progress so that you have a record of the changes in the way you feel and look. The following pages are split to suit either approach. If you are trying new recipes on a daily basis, use the 'My Juicy Lifestyle' log to note your stats, exercise taken and how the juices fit into your day. If you are cutting out all solids, use the 'My Juice Cleanse' log to note down how you are feeling – physically and mentally – and what results you achieve. It will help to tailor the juicing days to your own requirements so that you are well armed for the next cleanse you undertake.

My Juicy Lifestyle

Week 1

	Body stats
Weight:	
Chest measurement:	
Waist:	
Hips:	
Thigh:	
Upper arm:	
Body fat % (if known):	

	Juices tried this week		
Page:	When:		Rating:
Page:	When:		Rating:
Page:	When:		Rating:
Page:	When:		Rating:
Page:	When:		Rating:
Page:	When:		Rating:
Page:	When:		Rating:

Exercise log

My Juicy Lifestyle

Week 2

	Body stats
Weight:	
Chest measurement:	
Waist:	
Hips:	
Thigh:	
Upper arm:	
Body fat % (if known):	

Juices tried this week		
Page:	When:	Rating:
Page:	When:	Rating:
Page:	When:	Rating:
Page:	When:	Rating:
Page:	When:	Rating:
Page:	When:	Rating:
Page:	When:	Rating:

Exercise log

My Juicy Lifestyle

Week 3

	Body stats
Weight:	
Chest measurement:	
Waist:	
Hips:	
Thigh:	
Upper arm:	
Body fat % (if known):	

Juices tried this week		
Page:	When:	Rating:
Page:	When:	Rating:
Page:	When:	Rating:
Page:	When:	Rating:
Page:	When:	Rating:
Page:	When:	Rating:
Page:	When:	Rating:

Exercise log

My Juicy Lifestyle

Week 4

	Body stats
Weight:	
Chest measurement:	
Waist:	
Hips:	
Thigh:	
Upper arm:	
Body fat % (if known):	

Juices tried this week			
Page:	When:		Rating:
Page:	When:		Rating:
Page:	When:		Rating:
Page:	When:		Rating:
Page:	When:		Rating:
Page:	When:		Rating:
Page:	When:		Rating:

Exercise log

My Juicy Lifestyle

Week 5

	Body stats
Weight:	
Chest measurement:	
Waist:	
Hips:	
Thigh:	
Upper arm:	
Body fat % (if known):	

Juices tried this week			
Page:	When:		Rating:
Page:	When:		Rating:
Page:	When:		Rating:
Page:	When:		Rating:
Page:	When:		Rating:
Page:	When:		Rating:
Page:	When:		Rating:

Exercise log

My Juicy Lifestyle

Week 6

	Body stats
Weight:	
Chest measurement:	
Waist:	
Hips:	
Thigh:	
Upper arm:	
Body fat % (if known):	

Juices tried this week		
Page:	When:	Rating:
Page:	When:	Rating:
Page:	When:	Rating:
Page:	When:	Rating:
Page:	When:	Rating:
Page:	When:	Rating:
Page:	When:	Rating:

Exercise log

My Juicy Lifestyle

Week 7

	Body stats
Weight:	
Chest measurement:	
Waist:	
Hips:	
Thigh:	
Upper arm:	
Body fat % (if known):	

	Juices tried this week		
Page:	When:		Rating:
Page:	When:		Rating:
Page:	When:		Rating:
Page:	When:		Rating:
Page:	When:		Rating:
Page:	When:		Rating:
Page:	When:		Rating:

Exercise log

My Juicy Lifestyle

Week 8

	Body stats
Weight:	
Chest measurement:	
Waist:	
Hips:	
Thigh:	
Upper arm:	
Body fat % (if known):	

Juices tried this week		
Page:	When:	Rating:
Page:	When:	Rating:
Page:	When:	Rating:
Page:	When:	Rating:
Page:	When:	Rating:
Page:	When:	Rating:
Page:	When:	Rating:

Exercise log

Chart 1

My Juice Cleanse

Target number of
juice-only days:

	Pre-juice	Post-juice
Weight:		
Chest measurement:		
Waist:		
Hips:		
Thigh:		
Upper arm:		
Body fat % (if known):		

Before

How do you feel?

What do you hope to achieve by juicing?

What preparation have you done?

After

How do you feel?

What has improved the most?

What habits will you continue?

During

How do you feel?

What is proving hardest?

What are you enjoying?

Exercise log

Juices you liked

Chart 2

My Juice Cleanse

Target number of juice-only days:		

	Pre-juice	Post-juice
Weight:		
Chest measurement:		
Waist:		
Hips:		
Thigh:		
Upper arm:		
Body fat % (if known):		

Before

How do you feel?

What do you hope to achieve by juicing?

What preparation have you done?

During

How do you feel?

What is proving hardest?

What are you enjoying?

After

How do you feel?

What has improved the most?

What habits will you continue?

Exercise log

Juices you liked

Chart 3

My Juice Cleanse

Target number of juice-only days:		

	Pre-juice	Post-juice
Weight:		
Chest measurement:		
Waist:		
Hips:		
Thigh:		
Upper arm:		
Body fat % (if known):		

Before

How do you feel?

What do you hope to achieve by juicing?

What preparation have you done?

After

How do you feel?

What has improved the most?

What habits will you continue?

During

How do you feel?

What is proving hardest?

What are you enjoying?

Exercise log

Juices you liked

Take It Away

So, how do you feel? Hopefully you are now full of the joys of spring greens and can really appreciate the benefits brought by adding more fruit and vegetables to your life, and in such a quick, easy way.

Don't forget that a juice cleanse will take its toll on your appetite and on your body's ability to handle solid foods. Heed the warnings and do not dive straight back into a plateful of fish and chips or a full Chinese banquet – your digestive system will not cope.

Instead, ease your way back into eating with delicious salad-based meals, home-made soups and your chosen recipes from this book. Get your teeth into fresh, organic fruits straight from the bowl – no juicing required. Treat yourself to the very best ingredients and you should find that your taste buds crave distinctive tastes, not artificial ingredients – because now they know the difference.

Change the way you think about convenience food. A takeaway is not a reward; it is a step back to your old pre-juicing way of life. It is actually much quicker to fire up your juicer and give your body a proper present, gift-wrapped in a glass. Try to make juicing a daily habit, working your way through the recipes in this book according to your whims at the time. A glowing exterior and healthier insides will be the reward you truly deserve!

Diet consultant: Jo Stimpson.

Main food photography and recipe development: © StockFood.

All other recipe images courtesy of © Thinkstock, © Getty Images.